Kingdom Ambassadors' TOOLKIT

Kingdom Thinking

Angelo E. Quinlan

New Harvest Time
PUBLICATIONS

Published by New Harvest Time Publications

Copyright © 2017 Angelo E. Quinlan
All rights reserved. No part of this book may
be reproduced, stored, or transmitted by any
means—whether auditory, graphic, mechanical, or
electronic—without written permission of both publisher
and author, except in the case of brief excerpts used in
critical articles and reviews. Unauthorized reproduction
of any part of this work is illegal
and is punishable by law.

ISBN: 978-0-9991777-2-3 (Paperback)

Printed in the U.S.A.

Book Design by DesignForBooks.com

Contents

Introduction 1

Kingdom Purpose, Objective, and Assignment

Workshop/Seminar Toolkit – Phase One

Pages 3-6 – Kingdom Toolkit Review lessons 1-14

Understanding the N.E.T. Outreach System

Workshop/Seminar Toolkit – Phase Two

Pages 7-11 – Kingdom Toolkit Review Lessons 1-17

The Ambassadors of Christ - Part One

Workshop/Seminar Toolkit – Phase Three

Pages 13-16 – Kingdom Toolkit Review Lessons 1-8

The Ambassadors of Christ – Part Two

Workshop/Seminar Toolkit – Phase Four

Pages 17-21 – Kingdom Toolkit Review Lessons 1-14

The Ambassador's Creed

Page 23

Answer Codes 32

Introduction

The *Kingdom Ambassadors Toolkit* is an exercise program that promotes kingdom thinking that will ignite an outreach explosion in both the child of God as well as your city. It will generate personal excitement as well as personal expectations. The scriptural understanding taught in these seminars/workshops will reveal Christ's revelations of desires to greatly use every individual in the congregation. There will be a common excitement and anticipation among the body concerning the harvest Jesus promised to the laborers of the fields. The congregation will understand their personal divine part in this explosion, and they will contribute with great joy.

This training exercise program will reveal scriptural principles that enlighten Spirit-filled people concerning the Kingdom gifts God has placed in every believer by his Spirit. This eye-opening training will cause excitement in the Body of Christ. God will divulge the greatness he has placed within his Kingdom ambassadors. The Spirit of Christ will disclose that he has structured the body of Christ to work together with Christ to win the world. Implementing this building program will impact and bless the church congregation, along with the members' homes, their communities, and places of employment. This program will cause the angels to greatly rejoice and the Lord to say, "Well done, my good and faithful servants."

Kingdom Purpose, Objective, and Assignment

Workshop/Seminar Toolkit – Phase One

True & false and multiple choice. Select one.

1. What was the ultimate reason for Jesus' choosing the cross?

    - ☐ He prayed in the garden about it.
    - ☐ The cross was his Father's will.
    - ☐ He loved his apostles and followers.
    - ☐ None of the above.

2. Obedience is significant in cultivating an acceptable relationship with Christ?

    - ☐ True.
    - ☐ False.
    - ☐ Maybe.

3. What was the ultimate objective of Jesus' dying on the cross?

    - ☐ To bless all who would give their lives to him.
    - ☐ So that men and women might have salvation.
    - ☐ To pay the acceptable price for the forgiveness of the sins of mankind.
    - ☐ None of the above.

4. What is your personal responsibility in maintaining your salvation?

    ☐ Yielding my mind and my members unto Christ.
    ☐ Casting down thoughts and imaginations that would interfere with Christ's having access to my mind.
    ☐ Maintaining a heathy environment that will allow me to hear the voice of the Lord?
    ☐ All the above.

5. I have the authority and power to yield my mind to Christ as instruments for his glory.

    ☐ True.
    ☐ False.
    ☐ Sometimes.

6. What should be our main objective for each day?

    ☐ To be available instruments to Christ for his service daily.
    ☐ To praise his name every opportunity we get.
    ☐ To tell everyone how much God has blessed us.
    ☐ None of the above.

7. The personal battle of sin is a constant attack of the flesh against the mind . . .

    ☐ Starting with the beginning of each day.
    ☐ Only when the mind is meditating on evil thoughts.
    ☐ While you are sleeping and resting for the day to come.
    ☐ None of the above.

8 Do we have power to yield ourselves to Christ?

- ☐ Yes.
- ☐ No.
- ☐ Maybe.

9 What is Christ's ultimate hope to receive from our lives?

- ☐ To yield ourselves daily as his temple for his glory.
- ☐ That we might die daily, allowing Christ do his designed work within us.
- ☐ To showcase us as his workmanship to the world.
- ☐ All the above.

10 What should be our final objective at the end of each day?

- ☐ To review our service that we have rendered unto the Lord for the day.
- ☐ Count our many blessings, naming them one by one.
- ☐ Thank the Lord for his hand of divine protection.
- ☐ All the above.

11 What should be our ultimate purpose as a child of God?

- ☐ To be sensitive to the voice of the Lord throughout the day.
- ☐ To conduct ourselves as Kingdom children of God.
- ☐ To take every opportunity to share Christ when doors of opportunities become available.
- ☐ All of the above.

12 Everyone who is a new creature is part of God's outreach system?

- ☐ True.
- ☐ False.
- ☐ Only a few.

13 All those who are called by God are chosen to win souls?

- ☐ True.
- ☐ False.

14 All those who are filled with the Holy Ghost are anointed and called to win souls?

- ☐ True.
- ☐ False.
- ☐ Sometimes.

NOTES: _____
_____
_____
_____
_____
_____
_____
_____
_____
_____

Understanding the N.E.T. Outreach System

Workshop/Seminar Toolkit – Phase Two

True & false and multiple choice. Select one.

1. Working together with God to win the world.

    - ☐ This is the mindset that the whole body of Christ must understand to win souls.
    - ☐ It's necessary that just a few understand the call to work with God to win the world.
    - ☐ Only those with ministerial credentials are chosen to work with God in winning souls.
    - ☐ All the above.

2. Networking Evangelistic Team (N.E.T.)

    - ☐ Every man in Christ Jesus is part of the N.E.T.
    - ☐ All of the saints of God are part of the N.E.T.
    - ☐ Everyone is a fisherman of men and part of the N.E.T.
    - ☐ All the above are part of the N.E.T.

3. What services provide personal strength, educate, and care for the body of Christ, building fellowship as God's Kingdom N.E.T.?

    - ☐ Bible study.
    - ☐ Personal and group prayer.

- ☐ Daily reading and studying.
- ☐ Sunday morning services.
- ☐ Group fellowship gatherings.
- ☐ Personal fasting for direction.
- ☐ Select *only* the most important ones.

> *Use questions 4, 5, and 6 for open dialogue concerning the type of kingdom fishing Jesus spoke about.*

4 Net mending is the equipping of the Members

"And going on from thence, he saw other two brethren, James the son of Zebedee, and John his brother, in a ship with Zebedee their father, *mending their nets*; and he called them. And they immediately left the ship and their father, and followed him." (Matt 4:21–22 KJV)

5 Net cleaning (Prayer) is personal and corporate:

"[Jesus] saw two ships standing by the lake: but the fishermen were gone out of them, and were washing their nets. And he entered into one of the ships, which was Simon's, and prayed him that he would thrust out a little from the land. And he sat down, and taught the people out of the ship." (Luke 5:2–3 KJV)

6 NET casting (benediction) is the conclusion of every church service.

"And Jesus, walking by the sea of Galilee, saw two brethren, Simon called Peter, and Andrew his brother, casting a net into the sea: for they were fishers. And he saith unto them, Follow me, and I will make you fishers of men. And they straightway left their nets, and followed him." (Matt 4:18–20 KJV)

Discovering the Plentiful Harvest (Lost Souls)

7 Jesus told them, "The harvest is plentiful, but the workers are few." What did Jesus instruct them to do?

- ☐ To have prayer and fasting shut-ins asking the of the harvest to send souls.
- ☐ To pray that the Lord would send out workers to harvest the fields.
- ☐ Have musical workshops and concerts.
- ☐ Have fellowship dinners and free gifts.

8 How many souls have visited your services this month?

- ☐ None.
- ☐ A few.
- ☐ I will find out this month.

9 How many opportunities have you had to minister to a co-worker or friend?

- ☐ Every time a door is opened.
- ☐ A few.
- ☐ I don't remember.

10 How many people in your neighborhood or community know that you and your church are praying for your neighborhood and community?

- ☐ None.
- ☐ A few.
- ☐ Haven't asked everyone yet.

11 How many visitors who have visited any of your church services for the first time have you personally visited?

- ☐ None.
- ☐ A few.

12 Can you see that God has begun to send this church a part of the promised harvest, when you look at the number of visitors?

- ☐ Yes.
- ☐ No.

Releasing a Few More Laborers

13 Are you ready to give the Lord service in the fields?

- ☐ Yes.
- ☐ No.

14 Do you understand that everyone in the body has an assignment in the soul-winning system of God?

- ☐ Yes.
- ☐ No.

15 Do you understand that keeping track by visiting the souls who visit our church is how we collectively work together with God to win the world?

- ☐ Yes.
- ☐ No.

16 Do you understand this is how ambassadors show gratitude to the Lord for what He has done in their personal lives?

☐ Yes.
☐ No.

NOTES: _____
_____
_____
_____
_____
_____
_____
_____
_____
_____
_____
_____
_____
_____
_____
_____
_____
_____

The Ambassadors of Christ – Part One

Workshop/Seminar Toolkit – Phase Three

True & false and multiple choice. Select one.

The apostle Paul writes in the letter to the church in Ephesus concerning the divine structures, purpose, and objective of God's given leadership to the body of Christ: ". . . he gave some, apostles; and some, prophets; and some, evangelists; and some, pastors and teachers." Then God reveals why he gave them: "For the perfecting of the saints, for the work of the ministry, for the edifying of the body of Christ" (Ephesians 4:11–12 KJV).

God gave these to perfect the saints for their Kingdom assignments. Teaching the saints to work the ministry of Christ in the earth so that the body of Christ would be edified. Then Paul reminds all of the saints of God, who had been trained through the teachings of Jesus, apostles, prophets, evangelists, pastors, and teachers, "If any man be in Christ, he is a new creature: old things are passed away; behold, all things are become new. And all things are of God, who hath reconciled us to himself by Jesus Christ, and hath given to us the ministry of reconciliation making them ambassadors of Christ" (2 Corinthians 5:17–18, 20 KJV).

The Networking Evangelistic Team (N.E.T.) Body of Christ System

1. If any man be in Christ, he is a new creature. Who is the apostle Paul referring to in this verse (2 Corinthians 5:17)?

- ☐ Everyone who repents, receives the Holy Ghost, and gives their lives to Christ.
- ☐ Those who are ambassadors of Christ.
- ☐ The saints of God.
- ☐ All of the above.

2. What old things are passed away; and what things have become new (2 Corinthians 5:17)?

- ☐ Our sensitivity concerning the way we used to live our lives in sin is different.
- ☐ Now, as new creatures, we want to live for Christ and please him.
- ☐ Now we are open to the leading and guidance of the Holy Spirit.
- ☐ All of the above.

3. Which of these things could be some of both old and new things being referred to in this verse (2 Corinthians 5:17)?

- ☐ We abandon our old way of living and thinking about life.

- ☐ We are consumed with wanting to please Christ Jesus by doing his will.
- ☐ We have been forgiven from sin, and are now new creatures in the Kingdom of Christ.
- ☐ All of the above and more.

4 What does "all things are of God" refer to in this scripture (2 Corinthians 5:18)?

- ☐ God's hand of mercy was upon my life while I was yet lost in sin, until the day that I would give him my life, to become his masterpiece for his glory to the world.
- ☐ I am God's manifestation of his glory because he brought me out of darkness into his glorious likeness.
- ☐ Christ died for me when I was lost and rejected his love, mercy, grace, and the gift of eternal life.
- ☐ All of the above and more.

5 Who has reconciled us to himself by Jesus Christ?

- ☐ The Holy Spirit.
- ☐ The Father of Jesus Christ.
- ☐ Jesus Christ himself.
- ☐ All of the above.

6 Who has given us the ministry of reconciliation?

- ☐ The Father.
- ☐ The Son.
- ☐ The Holy Ghost.
- ☐ None of the above.

7 Whom has the ministry of reconciliation been given to?

- ☐ The apostles.
- ☐ The prophets.
- ☐ The ambassadors.
- ☐ All the saints.

8 To represent as an ambassador, you must…

- ☐ be a citizen of the country that you are representing.
- ☐ abide in another country other than the country you are a citizen of.
- ☐ be appointed by the king or government to represent said kingdom.
- ☐ All the above.

NOTES: _____
_____
_____
_____
_____
_____
_____
_____
_____
_____
_____

The Ambassadors of Christ – Part Two

Workshop/Seminar Toolkit – Phase Four

True & false and multiple choice. Select one.

1. The ambassador is given power and authority by the King to do business in another country on the King's behalf . . .

    - ☐ only in the country assignd to represent the King.
    - ☐ only in the country of his citizenship.
    - ☐ only when the citizens of the country the ambassador has been sent to allow him.
    - ☐ All the above.

2. The ambassador is representing the King and his Kingdom . . .

    - ☐ whenever doing business on the King's behalf.
    - ☐ only when invited to be in attendance of any meeting or gathering.
    - ☐ every hour of the day.
    - ☐ None of the above.

3. As an ambassador you can't officially represent in the country of your citizenship?

    - ☐ True.
    - ☐ False.

4 What is the ministry of reconciliation?

- ☐ The sharing with others how much God loves them and gave his son for them so that they might have eternal life.
- ☐ The ministry of reconciliation is the ability to share your personal story of how God restored your relationship with God through Jesus Christ.
- ☐ Sharing the story of how Christ made a way for men and women to have peace with God. Letting them know that he will do the same for others.
- ☐ Telling the story of how you repented and gave your life to Jesus, and he forgave you.
- ☐ All of the above.

5 What does "not imputing their trespasses unto them" mean?

- ☐ To not forgive them of their trespasses.
- ☐ To hold it against them until they do better.
- ☐ To forget about them until the catching away.
- ☐ To blot out their sins and remember them no more.

6 The King provides all of the ambassador's economic and personal needs while representing the King in another country?

- ☐ True.
- ☐ False.

7 Can you be an ambassador of the Kingdom of Christ if your citizenship is still of the world?

- ☐ Yes, you can.
- ☐ No, you can't.

8 Which one of the statements below is not necessary to be an ambassador of Christ?

- ☐ Be born-again of the Spirit.
- ☐ Be a citizen of the Kingdom of God.
- ☐ Be a new creature in Christ Jesus.
- ☐ Be a faithful church member and tithe payer.

9 Why is understanding the scriptures important to the believers of Christ?

- ☐ So they will be able to give an account of their hopes to anyone who asks them.
- ☐ So their pastors will see that they are faithful and dependable.
- ☐ So the deacons might see them and encourage them to continue to be faithful.
- ☐ All of the above.

10 Who has been given the word of reconciliation?

- ☐ Only the apostles and prophets.
- ☐ All the elders, teachers, and evangelists.
- ☐ Every new creature in Christ Jesus.
- ☐ Only those called to be ambassadors of Christ.

11 What is the word of reconciliation?

- ☐ The personal story of how Christ reconciled you.
- ☐ The preaching of reconciliation from the gospel of Jesus Christ.
- ☐ The story of Jesus found in the Pauline epistles, the letters of apostle Paul.
- ☐ None of the above.

12 Who are the ambassadors for Christ?

- ☐ Those who have been in Christ Jesus for at least one year.
- ☐ Only those who finish and pass the ambassador classes.
- ☐ All the new creatures in Christ Jesus.
- ☐ All the above.

13 According to this chapter, what are the necessary credentials to be an ambassador of Christ?

- ☐ Must finish and pass the minister classes.
- ☐ Must be a new creature in Christ Jesus.
- ☐ Must have been a member of the church for at least a year.
- ☐ None of the above.

14 Who is to be reconciled to God? And how are those who are reconciled to God to remain reconciled?

- ☐ Constant repentance and requests for forgiveness.
- ☐ Endless prayer for guidance.
- ☐ Praying in the Holy Ghost.
- ☐ All of the above.

NOTES:

The Ambassador's Creed

Knowledge - A Spiritual Mind

Kingdom ambassadors must have knowledge of the born-again experiences and understanding of the power of reconciliation. They must have knowledge of the character, mind, and purposes of the love of God toward men and the Kingdom of God on the earth.

Wisdom — A Humble Method

Ambassadors must remember that the Lord has been gracious, merciful, and kind unto them. This knowledge must be deployed in a skillful and passionate way, seasoned with grace. They must request that the wisdom of the Spirit enables them to stay mindful of those still trapped in sinful lives, and pray that the Spirit opens the eyes of their minds that they might see this glorious gospel. Touch them to ask for forgiveness. Anoint them by your Spirit to make this message of salvation convincing.

Character — A Beautiful, Attractive Spirit

Because Kingdom ambassadors represents Christ in everything they do, their personal maturity and individual virtue can draw souls to Christ or turn them away. They are always to be prayerful concerning their personal behavior and the gospel of forgiveness in their message about their Savior Jesus Christ.

8. Which of the statements below is not necessary to be an ambassador of Christ?

   ▶ Be a faithful church member and tithe payer.

9. Why is understanding the scriptures important to the believers of Christ?

   ▶ So they will be able to give an account of their hope to anyone who asks them.

10. Who has been given the word of reconciliation?

    ▶ Every new creature in Christ Jesus.

11. What is the word of reconciliation?

    ▶ The personal story of how Christ reconciled you.

12. Who are the ambassadors for Christ?

    ▶ All the new creatures in Christ Jesus.

13. According to this chapter, what are the necessary credentials to be an ambassador of Christ?

    ▶ Must be a new creature in Christ Jesus.

14. And how are those who are reconciled to God to remain reconciled?

    ▶ All of the above.

The Ambassadors of Christ – Part Two

Workshop/Seminar Toolkit – Phase Four

1. The ambassador is given power and authority by the King to do business in another country on the King's behalf…

   ▶ only in the country assign to represent the King.

2. The ambassador is representing the King and his Kingdom…

   ▶ every hour of the day.

3. As an ambassador you can't officially represent in the country of your citizenship.

   ▶ True.

4. What is the ministry of reconciliation?

   ▶ All of the above.

5. What does "not imputing their trespasses unto them" mean?

   ▶ To blot out their sins and remember them no more.

6. The King provides all of the ambassador's economic and personal needs while representing the King in another country.

   ▶ True.

7. Can you be an Ambassador of the Kingdom of Christ if your citizenship is still of the world?

   ▶ No, you can't.

Answer Codes

7. Whom has the ministry of reconciliation been given to?

   ▶ All the Saints.

8. To represent as an ambassador you must...

   ▶ All of the above.

The Ambassadors of Christ - Part One

Workshop/Seminar Toolkit – Phase Three

The Networking Evangelistic Team (N.E.T.) Body of Christ System

1. If any man be in Christ, he is a new creature. Who is the apostle Paul referring to in this verse (2 Corinthians 5:17)?
   - ▶ Everyone who repents, receives the Holy Ghost, and gives their lives to Christ.

2. What old things are passed away and what things have become new (2 Corinthians 5:17)?
   - ▶ All of the above.

3. Which of these things could be some of both old and new things being referred to in this verse (2 Corinthians 5:17)?
   - ▶ All of the above and more.

4. What does "all things are of God" refer to in this scripture (2 Corinthians 5:18)?
   - ▶ All of the above and more.

5. Who has reconciled us to himself by Jesus Christ?
   - ▶ The Father of Jesus Christ.

6. Who has given us the ministry of reconciliation
   - ▶ The Father.

11. How many visitors who have visited any of your church services for the first time have you personally visited?

   ▶ None.

   ▶ A few.

12. Can you see that God has begun to send this church a part of the promised harvest, when you look at the number of visitors?

   ▶ Yes.

Releasing a Few
re Laborers

13. Are you ready to give the Lord service in the fields?

   ▶ Yes.

14. Do you understand that everyone in the body has an assignment in the soul-winning system of God?

   ▶ Yes.

15. Do you understand that keeping track by visiting the souls that visit our church is how we collectively work together with God to win the world?

   ▶ Yes.

16. Do you understand this is how ambassadors show gratitude to the Lord for what he has done in our personal lives?

   ▶ Yes.

gone out of them, and were washing their nets. And he entered into one of the ships, which was Simon's, and prayed him that he would thrust out a little from the land. And he sat down, and taught the people out of the ship." (Luke 5:2–3 KJV)

6. N.E.T. casting (benediction) is the conclusion of every church service.

"And Jesus, walking by the sea of Galilee, saw two brethren, Simon called Peter, and Andrew his brother, casting a net into the sea: for they were fishers. And he saith unto them, Follow me, and I will make you fishers of men. And they straightway left their nets, and followed him." (Matt 4:18–20 KJV)

Discovering the Plentiful Harvest (Lost Souls)

7. Jesus told them "The harvest is plentiful, but the workers are few." What did Jesus instruct them to do?

   ▶ To pray that the Lord would send out workers to harvest the fields.

8. How many souls have visited your services this month?

   ▶ I will find out this month.

9. How many opportunities have you had to minister to a co-worker or friend?

   ▶ Every time a door is opened.

10. How many people in your neighborhood or community know that you and your church are praying for your neighborhood and community?

   ▶ Haven't asked everyone yet.

Understanding the N.E.T. Outreach System

Workshop/Seminar Toolkit – Phase Two

1. Working Together with God to Win the World.

   ▶ This is the mindset that the whole body of
     Christ must understand to win souls.

2. Networking Evangelistic Team (N.E.T.)

   ▶ All the above are part of the N.E.T.

3. What services provide personal strength,, education, and care for
   the body of Christ, building fellowship as God's Kingdom N.E.T.?

   ▶ Bible study.

   ▶ Personal and group prayer.

   ▶ Daily reading and studying.

   ▶ Sunday morning services.

   ▶ Group fellowship gatherings.

   ▶ Personal fasting for direction.

4. Net mending is the equipping of the members.

   "And going on from thence, he saw other two brethren, James
   the son of Zebedee, and John his brother, in a ship with Zebedee
   their father, mending their nets; and he called them. And they
   immediately left the ship and their father, and followed him."
   (Matt 4:21–22 KJV)

5. Net cleaning (Prayer) is personal.

   "[Jesus] saw two ships standing by the lake: but the fishermen were

7. The personal battle of sin is a constant attack of the flesh against the mind . . .

▶ starting with the beginning of each day.

8. Do we have power to yield ourselves to Christ?

▶ Yes.

9. What is Christ's ultimate hope to receive from our lives?

▶ All the above.

10. What should be our final objective at the end of each day?

▶ To review our service that we have rendered unto the Lord for the day.

11. What should be our ultimate purpose as children of God?

▶ All of the above.

12. Everyone who is a new creature is part of God's Outreach System.

▶ True.

13. All those who are called by God are chosen to win souls.

▶ True.

14. All those who are filled with the Holy Ghost are anointed and called to win souls.

▶ True.

A

ANSWER CODES

Kingdom Purpose, Objective, and Assignment

Workshop/Seminar Toolkit – Phase One

1. What was the ultimate reason for Jesus' choosing the cross?

    ▶ It was his father's will.

2. Obedience is significant in cultivating an acceptable relationship with Christ.

    ▶ True.

3. What was the ultimate objective of Jesus' dying on the cross?

    ▶ To pay the acceptable price for the forgiveness of the sins of mankind.

4. What is your personal responsibility in maintaining your Salvation?

    ▶ All the above.

5. I have the authority and power to yield my mind to Christ as his instrument for his glory.

    ▶ True.

6. What should be our main objective for each day?

    ▶ To be available instruments to Christ for service daily.

www.ingramcontent.com/pod-product-compliance
Lightning Source LLC
Chambersburg PA
CBHW080519020526
44113CB00055B/2534